THE
TRIALS AND TRIBULATIONS
OF THE
TRAUMATIZED TRAVELER

Why Me?

KEVIN B. KINNEE

Distributed by:
K & JK Inc
1052 VBL Estates B-4
Greencastle In. 46135
(765) 739-6332
kkinnee@ccrtc.com

This book is reality. The situations described within happened to me while traveling on the lecture circuit. Only the names have been changed to protect the idiots.

POLITICALLY CORRECTNESS:

For it seems my whole life I have had a cloud over me. Every where I go people say, *"If something is going to go wrong it will happen to Kevin."* This book is a direct result of that assumption. I write what I see at airports and hotels. Michelle read the book in an early form and made the comment that at times my observations bordered on cruel.

FOR THE RECORD:

I am a short, fat, bald guy with no neck who happens to be a disabled veteran. This allows me the ability to observe and critique society without being politically incorrect. My suggestion is to take this book and my observations as satire and humor. It is not a personal assault, it is a mirror of society.

Dedication

I dedicate this book to my wife, Janet, who after 24 years has just about got me trained, and to my three sons, who even though they have moved out, still drop by for their weekly allowance.

I would also like to thank my mom, Ellen Jane Kinnee, for her help.

Thanks to Jim Alsup for placing me in harms way so I would have something to write about.

Why Me?

WHY IS IT?

The guy seated next to me has nose hairs that are braided into a rope?

WHY IS IT?

When traveling by car, I will only get cramps and the urge to go to the bathroom when the next exit is 50 miles away?

WHY IS IT?

I am always stuck next to a screaming newborn who waits UNTIL takeoff to poop mustard?

WHY IS IT?

The mother of the mustard pooper has to sing to quiet the kid down?

WHY IS IT?

The mother couldn't carry a tune in a bucket?

WHY IS IT?

Everyone from the stewardesses to the passengers thinks she is my wife and they hate me for it?

WHY IS IT?

When babies poop mustard, they make little fists next to their heads to signal that it has begun?

WHY IS IT?

They have to sound like a small engine that needs a tune up?

WHY IS IT?

I am always stuck next to a nose picker on the plane?

WHY IS IT?

When you exit your aircraft they tell you where your connecting gate is, knowing full well they will change the gate before you get there?

WHY IS IT?

There is always someone who can't tell that their 2000 pound bag will not fit under the seat or in the overhead compartment of the plane?

WHY IS IT?

When the passenger is confronted about the bag they plead ignorance? They should take the bag, drop it from the emergency exit to the ground and sling it up into the cargo bay. Maybe this will teach them a lesson.

WHY IS IT?

There is always one person who sits in the airport for hours, only to board the plane and then have to go to the bathroom?

WHY ME?

While lecturing in Tennessee a ceiling tile dropped on my head and I was drenched with water. I went to the person in charge of maintenance for the hotel and asked, what's the deal with the ceiling tile and water? He said "was it about 5 gallons of water"? I stated yes. He looked at me and stated that I was lucky the bucket didn't hit me. He had discovered a roof leak so to solve it he placed a five gallon bucket on the ceiling tile to catch the water. When the bucket filled the tile gave way and the water and tile landed on my head. Lucky for me the bucket got caught or I might have been squashed like a toad on the highway.

WHY ME?

My wife and I were on our second leg of a trip when we stopped for a quiet dinner. We sat down and the waitress stated that the featured meal was the T-bone dinner. So I asked, "how much is it?" She stated that it was the regular price. I asked, "why is it the same price as always"? She said "it's the featured meal and not a special." I began to wonder what the heck I had stumbled into. Behind me was seated an 80 year old man with no teeth. He kept turning around and looking over my shoulder at my wife. While he was staring he would wiggle his lips together making a squeaking sound. I began to feel like we were in an insane asylum. I asked my wife if she wanted me to move over to block his view of her. She stated no but I got the distinct feeling the older gentlemen took offense to my statement. He mumbled he was leaving and then stood and backed his buttocks up to within a foot of my head. I could not believe my ears. There it was the unmistakable putt-putt-putt of a long series fart. I reacted immediately by leaning away so the hair on my ears would not be singed. I turned as the old man walked off with a strut in his Bermuda shorts and black knee length multi-colored stretch socks. What are the odds of this happening to me! I guess this re-defines the terms, "OLD FART."

WHY IS IT?

They delay the planes departure until the person returns to their seat? The captain should take off when they are on the stool. Next time they might remember!!

WHY IS IT?

There is always one person who has a 2′ long bag turned sideways when they walk down the isle of the plane?

WHY IS IT?

The person with this bag always bangs me?

WHY IS IT?

After telling all the passengers to place their seat in the upright position, there is always one person who has to be singled out and told to do it? I think the stewardess should have the right to stab them in the head with a fork. Then when you see them wandering around the airport you would notice the forks and know this one was too stupid to follow directions.

4

WHY IS IT?

After telling the passengers that small portable electronics like tape players should not be used because it may affect the navigation gear of the aircraft, some people continue to use them. I think they should be asked to step outside.

WHY IS IT?

Some people will get pre-assigned window seats and then wait till last to board the plane?

WHY IS IT?

When the above person enters the plane they have 4 bags and no where to put them.

WHY IS IT?

They get mad when there is no room in the overhead compartment to put their bags?

WHY IS IT?

They always want to put their bag under the seat in front of me?

WHY IS IT?

They say excuse me, then won't step out of the way so you can exit the row to let them in?

WHY IS IT?

They always step on your feet, even though you give them enough room to turn a truck around?

WHY ME?

While preparing to lecture in Vegas, I plugged in two TV's and a VCR. When I turned them on this loud popping noise was emitted and smoke began to billow out of all three. I kicked out the plug and ran for my life. When nothing else happened I dismantled the fried equipment and replaced them with rentals. I turned them on and again they went up in smoke. I demanded to know what the heck was going on! I found that the electrician had wired a 110 circuit with 220 and didn't tell anyone.

WHY IS IT?

When there is one seat left on the plane and it's next to me, a 500 pound person will sit in it?

WHY IS IT?

He will get two drinks and chew the ice?

WHY IS IT?

I am always stuck next to the guy who takes his shoes off?

WHY IS IT?

This guy will have a big hole in his socks?

WHY IS IT?

This guys feet smell like a combination of Parmesan cheese and onions?

WHY IS IT?

This guy can be identified by his striped socks?

WHY IS IT?

This guy will always ask for extra peanuts? Like they are going to fill him up!!

WHY IS IT?

When this guy gets up, his butt is next to my face?

WHY IS IT?

This guy will always have a weggie?

WHY IS IT?

This guy will grab a hand full of underwear and pull them out of the crevice while you are a captive viewer?

WHY IS IT?

When this guy gets off the plane there is an 80 pound woman waiting for him?

WHY ME?

At 6:30 a.m. I boarded my plane for Houston only to find an extremely large woman in my seat. I had asked for an aisle seat so I could at least lean away from any adversity that was placed next to me. I informed her that she was in my seat. She went though the process of finding her ticket and in a disgusted manner forced herself to admit she was wrong. To my surprise she then stated that I could find another seat. I almost told her that I had no desire to sit next to her but I remembered that the person at check in stated it was a full flight. I also gaged my chance of survival in a wrestling match and realized that I would lose. So, because discretion is the better part of valor, I again asked her to move.

She struggled to her feet and I heard a squeak as her hips popped out of the chair. I sat in the chair and immediately became aware that something wet was left on the arms of the chair. I looked closer at the chair and observed a skin colored lotion smeared there. I looked at the women's arms and noticed for the first time that she had scabs on them. The lotion appeared to be treatment for what ever disease she had acquired. I obtained a blanket which I hastily put on the arms and then I settled in for the flight. As soon as I arrived at the hotel I ran in, stripped down and washed until I bled. The whole time wondering what I had done in a previous life to deserve all this adversity?

WHY IS IT?

When you get off the plane everyone hugs and kisses in the doorway of the exit?

WHY IS IT?

When you buy an item at a shop at the airport you will always find the same item cheaper in the next shop?

WHY IS IT?

So difficult to admit a mistake and take the item back to the first store?

WHY IS IT?

They price the nuts at the airport by the 1/2 pound?

WHY IS IT?

The nuts are $12 a pound?

DAAAAAA?

Jim and I arrived in Texas in the late afternoon so we went to a Mexican restaurant to get something to eat. We were waited on by a guy who was from New York. The waiter placed chips and salsa on the table in front of us. Before I ate I asked him if the salsa was mild and he responded yes. I dug in as Jim asked if they had any hot salsa for him? The waiter stated "sure I will get you some." He soon returned and placed a small bowl in front of Jim. Jim, being starved, dug in with vigor. I looked up as Jim let out a scream. The waiter looked at him and stated "You asked for hot salsa." Jim responded "Yes, but I didn't expect you to microwave it." I looked at Jim and stated "He said he was from New York"!

WHY ME?

I got on the plane early only to find that I was in for a unique ride. I watched as a husband and wife walked in. I also noted that they had a child. It was obvious that their family tree had no fork in it! They sat in front of me and began pulling out drinks from every conceivable hiding place on their bodies. They had four cokes and three milks when they finished. I was in an exit row so I decided to tell the stewardess that I could not perform the duties required to sit in an exit row. I felt it was better to be a wimp than be abused. As I started to get up the 1½ year old kid laid down across the aisle so I could not exit. I sat back resigned to my fate, when I noticed that the stewardess was handing out head phones. I decided to get a pair. It would be better to block out any adverse activity that they may provide. For the next three or four minutes I feared that she would run out of headphones before she reached me. At last she arrived and I grabbed the head phones as the child started making noises. I soon realized that the noises were not emanating from the facial area of the child. I soon began to detect a unique smell. I reached up and turned the air control over my seat hoping against all hope that they pilot had turned it on. As I suspected it was not. I began to concentrate on my head phones following all known procedures to get them to work. I pulled them off, looked for crimps and rotated the dials on the seat to no avail. I continued to work feverishly in the hopes that I could divert my concentration away from the child. By now we had taken off and were climbing so I again reached for the air and found to my surprise that it did in fact work. I turned it up full blast and began to receive my relief. At this time I heard the head phones stir to life. The first I heard was an apology from the pilots. They stated that they had forgotten to turn on the music. I settled back oblivious of the presence of the kid pooping mustard. I fell into a light sleep where all was calm and peaceful. I was jolted back to life by this all consuming wave of smell that took my breath away. I jerked upright and grabbed my nose. I looked around me only to see everyone holding their noses. I thought I was still sleeping and found myself in a bad movie. I was jolted back to reality as the husband leaned his seat back and I observed the worst fate that can confront an air traveler. The mother was in the process of changing the kids diaper. This activity just happened to coincide with the passing of the food cart. The parents stopped changing the diaper long enough to get two turkey sandwiches and two drinks. I could not believe my ears when the stewardess asked them if they wanted "mustard on it!"

WHY IS IT?

When you get a drink on the plane, they only give you half a can?

WHY IS IT?

My wife can demand the rest of the can and I won't?

WHY IS IT?

When I put fragile stickers all over my bag at check in, they are all rubbed and torn when I pick them up? (what would I find if the fragile stickers were not on it?)

WHY IS IT?

Everyone jumps up into the aisle when the plane stops at the gate? (do they think this will speed up their departure?)

WHY IS IT?

People will get off the plane and stop in the way and start messing with their carry on luggage?

WHY IS IT?

People try to carry luggage and an ice cream cone on the plane at the same time?

WHY IS IT?

I am always next to the one person on the plane who is air sick?

WHY IS IT?

When someone flies with me on a trip this stuff never happens?

WHY IS IT?

I have to fly 300 miles east to go west?

WHY IS IT?

You are never told your flight is canceled until you stand in line for an hour?

WHY IS IT?

You go to Florida but your bags go to New York?

WHY IS IT?

Air travel provides so many "Why Is It's" IS IT'S"?

WHY IS IT?

You see them handle your bags so carefully at check in, only to see them dropped off the truck as it is taken to the plane?

WHY IS IT?

You take a trip and the whole way it is sunshine, but when you arrive your bags are soaking wet?

WHY IS IT?

When you watch TV at the airport on a pay TV it seems to need more change during the best part of the show?

WHY ME?

When I was staying in Texas at a major hotel chain, I began to notice that everywhere I went they had the feeling that everything was bigger in Texas. I returned to my room not convinced. I went to the bathroom and sat on the throne. I picked up my bass book and waited for nature to take it's course. I was just about ready to find some relief when a sound permeates the bathroom. I looked around and saw nothing. The sound was like little running feet. I went back to reading when I again heard the sound. I stopped, looked around and then just as I was getting ready to take care of business something hit me on the head. I reached up, located the object, and began to remove it when it began to hiss and wiggle. I let out a yelp, slid off the seat and began to roll like I was on fire. I wrenched what ever it was from my hair and threw it at the wall. I heard a squeak and then a plop. I grabbed a shoe off the floor and crawled over to the object. To my amazement the object turned out to be a 4″ bug. I caught it in a drinking glass and it formed an "L" shape because it was too long to lay across the bottom of the glass. I dressed, indignant as hell and went plodding up to the reception desk. I demanded to see a manager. When he arrived I demanded to know how a 4″ roach had gotten into my room? The manager looked at the bug then at me and said "hell boy, that's just a water bug and a pretty small one at that." I stammered and stuttered for a second and then turned and walked away. What could I say! I guess things are bigger in Texas!!!!

WHY IS IT?

The "take a number" airline punishes late arrival by giving them a bulk head seat facing the crowd?

13

WHY IS IT?

We who are on the plane have to face the late arrival?

WHY IS IT?

I never get a connecting flight close to my arrival gate?

WHY IS IT?

When I am running to make my second connection, I run into an extended family? (extended from one side of the hall to the other)

WHY IS IT?

When I clear this group, I get stuck behind a person on a walker?

WHY IS IT?

When I eat at the airport, I always get stuck behind someone who pays with a credit card?

WHY IS IT?

The cashier that takes the card is always new and needs help with the transaction?

WHY ME?

I entered the aircraft as usual wondering what was going to go wrong. I felt that for once the trip may be a good one. I sat down in the emergency row and find that there was no one next to me. I was pretty happy until an elderly woman asked the stewardess if it was all right if she moved to the open seat next to me. She was given permission and then the move began. The women moved out into the aisle she was assigned and moved up and down the aisle stopping at three different overhead compartments. She removed her belongings and placed them up over me. She sat down in the window seat and I began to sit down and fasten my seat belt. I no more than got done and she remembers that she had another bag in a different overhead. I again got up as she gets the bag and moves it. I again sat and buckled up. She looked at me and asked me if I thought it was hot. I mumbled a response as she again excused herself. I got up and moved to the aisle as she placed her coat in the overhead. I waited until she re-seats herself and then I go through the process again. We take off and I drift off to sleep. I wake to a tug on my sleeve. She needed to go to the bathroom. I stepped out and she manages to walk on both of my feet. I look at my watch and find we have been in the air only ten minutes. I sat down and drifted off again. The next thing I am aware of is the little old lady getting in the overhead compartment. I open my eyes as a large dark object falls from the overhead. I realized that it was going to strike me in the head. I threw myself to the right to avoid the impact. When I reacted I heard a loud crunch and felt a searing pain in my neck. I spasmed in pain as the light weight jacket landed on me. The jacket looked huge as I came out of my nap and fell toward me. I started to laugh at the thought of how stupid my action must have looked. I then realized that my neck was locked to the right. I could move it but when I faced forward a sharp pain went through my chest and back. I could not believe I had pulled a muscle. I spent the next two days turning my body instead of my neck. All this because of a falling jacket.

WHY IS IT?

After you run the length of the airport and just barely make your flight, why is the flight then delayed for late arrival?

WHY IS IT?

When my plane is late they won't hold my connection?

WHY IS IT?

The person behind me has to press their feet into my back?

WHY IS IT?

No matter how far my gate is, I never get a ride on the airport golf carts?

WHY IS IT?

Babies can't be trained to poop before they get on the plane?

WHY IS IT?

The smell from the baby seems to be magnified on the plane?

WHY IS IT?

When you ride on a twin prop aircraft they instruct you in case of a fire to take the fire extinguisher from the wall and point it at the base of the flame and shoot? First off, I need to know how often is there a fire on a plane and second, do we fight the fire because the crew is going to run?

WHY IS IT?

When you have an early morning flight and you arrive as required one hour early, why is there no one at check in to wait on you?

WHY IS IT?

You are in a prop flying over the mountains and they come on the PA and state we are going to be delayed because we can't land in the rain? The time to tell me is before we take off!!!!!!!

WHY IS IT?

When you fly the twin props you notice all the patches on the aircraft?

WHY IS IT?

You also notice the patches are not painted? Is this because the patches don't last long enough to make painting worthwhile?

WHY IS IT?

I seem to get stuck next to the only passenger who can't speak English and why do they want to carry on a conversation for the whole flight?

WHY IS IT?

The food on the plane smells so good but tastes so bad?

WHY IS IT?

They don't have a tag on the food that is served so you at least have an idea what it is you are eating?

WHY IS IT?

I get stuck next to a person who has a nose full and they keep sniffing instead of blowing it?

WHY IS IT?

Passengers near me wait until I'M seated to start coughing on me and they stop when I get up?

WHY IS IT?

I get stuck next to a person with a skin disease and they are so big they constantly rub it against me?

WHY IS IT?

When I arrive for check in, wait in line, and finally get to the front the employee that was to wait on me goes on break?

WHY IS IT?

Airports have limited seating and some passengers put their bags on several seats?

WHY IS IT?

There are so many strange people at the airport?

WHY IS IT?

There seems to always be an elderly women who cuts in front of me in line at check in?

WHY IS IT?

This same woman, when asked why she cut in will say "I have an illness today?"

WHY IS IT?

You have to check in at the airport entrance and then you may be asked to check in also at the gate?

WHY IS IT?

They have a plane that holds 200 but a gate that seats only 12?

WHY IS IT?

When they announce that pre boarding will begin for people who are disabled, half the people that respond think that being stupid is a disability?

WHY IS IT?

People who have a seat assignment near the front of the aircraft and know that the loading begins at the rear will still rush to the gate and block the entrance?

WHY IS IT?

The only time a women carries three purses is when they get on an aircraft?

WHY IS IT?

People wait till the last minute to arrive at the airport then wonder why their bags don't make the flight?

WHY IS IT?

They have a size limit on bags but not people?

WHY IS IT?

People wait until they get on the plane before they look at their seat assignment?

WHY IS IT?

I get stuck near a guy who can't sit still? His arms are up most of the time and he has a hole in the armpit of his shirt.

WHY IS IT?

You hurry to get to your destination and you smile and think you will arrive early for once, they then taxi to a spot where the aircraft is held just long enough to make you late?

WHY IS IT?

After the stewardess informs us to keep our seat belts fastened until we reach the gate, there comes this clamor of seat belts opening?

WHY IS IT?

It's not until you begin to roll down the runway that you notice all the problems with the aircraft?

WHY ME?

I pull in and park my car in the long term parking lot. As I exit the car it starts to rain and I begin to think that this is going to be one of those bad experiences. I finally get to the terminal and found a very long line. I take my place and wait for the line to dwindle. As I got about two thirds of the way through the line an employee walks around the counter and calls for everyone going to Pittsburgh. I grabbed my bags and made a dash for the woman. I was now third in that line. She opened a line up and began to process us. I noticed that the two people in front of me had a heated discussion with the employee and then walked to the end of the original line. I was called up to the woman and she stated "Philadelphia"? I said no "you said Pittsburgh! She said I am sorry I meant Philadelphia. I turned around and noticed that the original line was now twice as long as it was before. I also noticed that the last person who could verify that I was in line before was now walking away. I walked back to the rear of the line just in time to see a little old lady place her bags under the rope near the front of the line. She walked back to where I was and requested that I move aside. I said excuse me and she said see those bags up there, those are mine and I need by. She then walked all the way from the rear to the front and stood there like she was born there. I could have said something or done something to her which would have made me feel better but all I could think of was the fact that this woman was probably being assigned the seat next to me!!!!

WHY IS IT?

I can't tell which is worse, fish tailing on takeoff or landing?

WHY IS IT?

People think they should have a drink service on a 20 minute flight?

WHY IS IT?

That airlines are allowed to call this food?

WHY IS IT?

Airlines are not required to have warning labels on their food?

WHY IS IT?

There is always one person on the flight that will scratch his head and then clean their nails with their teeth? This is like being at the zoo?

WHY IS IT?

They serve peanuts? Do we look like elephants? Wait don't answer that!

WHY IS IT?

That the guy next to me will turn on the overhead light then go to sleep and snore?

WHY IS IT?

I am always behind the two lovebirds who spend the whole trip swapping spit and getting chapped lips?

WHY IS IT?

People on standby get mad when they don't get a seat?

WHY IS IT?

So many people in first class take off their shoes?

WHY IS IT?

First class passengers look disgusted when the rest of us peons board the plane? If I was first class I would not be in a hurry to board.

WHY IS IT?

Many first class passengers remind you of the worst teacher you ever had?

WHY IS IT?

First class is at the front of the plane? You would think that since the front hits the ground first they would want to be in the back!

WHY IS IT?

When people in the back of the plane board, they put their luggage in the overheads at the front of the aircraft? There should be someone assigned to relocate their bags so they can never find them!!

WHY IS IT?

When you go to pick up your bags, some employee will start up the carousel and then stop it? This person needs to be bagged and tagged!

WHY IS IT?

The seven biggest people in the world seem to be between me and my bags?

WHY IS IT?

My bag is always the last one off the plane?

WHY IS IT?

If I check two bags in, one will come off the plane first and one will be last?

WHY IS IT?

You can check a new bag and an old bag and the one that will get damaged will be the new one? Is this called selective destruction?

WHY IS IT?

Airlines really do hire that gorilla to jump on the luggage? You don't have to convince me!!!!

WHY IS IT?

New York is the favorite destination for my bags? I have never been there but my bags have!!

WHY IS IT?

The only time your bags arrive early is when you are not in a hurry?

WHY IS IT?

The airlines don't have a definition written on their fragile stickers so the baggage people will know what it means? Maybe pictures would help!

WHY IS IT?

When I get ready to leave for the airport my family lines up with their hands out? I think they relate it to payday!

WHY IS IT?

I fly around the country to work and my family waits at home for the check?

WHY IS IT?

I have to bring them presents when I am the only one with a job?

WHY IS IT?

If it's not the weather it is the computers in Chicago that delays me?

WHY IS IT?

People will sit in the long term parking aisles for hours waiting for a closer parking place?

WHY IS IT?

When a passenger injures you with their bag they state "I am sorry, did I hurt you?" No dipshit this is fake blood!

WHY IS IT?

When you change your seat to an emergency row to get more room, they put a 400 pounder next to you?

WHY IS IT?

The plane I ride on is always the one with the squeaky brakes?

WHY IS IT?

When I locate a seat away from everyone and I settle in to relax, someone always brings their uncontrolled kids over to sit by me?

WHY IS IT?

No matter what line I get in, it will stop halfway through it?

WHY IS IT?

I always get in a line where there is someone in training?

WHY IS IT?

There are 6 check in positions and they only have one attendant?

WHY IS IT?

They want you to check in early to be on the standby list and then they don't put you on the list?

WHY IS IT?

They wait till the last minute to tell you that all the seats are filled?

WHY IS IT?

They say you are 5th on the standby list, they call seven names and you are not one of them?

WHY IS IT?

You have 118 seats on the plane and they book 134 passengers?

WHY IS IT?

They announce that all passengers must board so they can take a seat count, and there are always several passengers that don't comply?

WHY IS IT?

When you need to eat something at the airport, all that is there is pizza?

WHY IS IT?

You never learn that airport pizza is designed to destroy your intestines?

WHY IS IT?

Airport food is not required to post warning labels?

WHY IS IT?

People will complain about a bed at a hotel but they don't think anything about sleeping on the floor at the airport?

WHY IS IT?

You don't see more domestic violence at the airports?

WHY IS IT?

So many of the airport police you see are seasoned citizens?

WHY IS IT?

A stewardess can get their clothes in one small bag but my wife has to have five?

WHY IS IT?

Amish don't use cars but you see them at the Chicago airport?

WHY IS IT?

They provide you with a toilet seat cover but they don't tell you how to keep it on the seat?

WHY IS IT?

Elderly men wear shorts and knee socks at the airport?

WHY IS IT?

People put their tickets in their backpacks and then search their pockets because they forgot they had a backpack on?

WHY IS IT?

Fat women wear bright colored stretch pants at the airport?

WHY IS IT?

People will carry 4 little bags instead of consolidating them into one big one?

WHY IS IT?

Airport ground personnel wear ear protection inside the airport?

WHY IS IT?

They don't give us ear plugs when boarding props.

WHY IS IT?

Black motorcycle boots on a woman makes you think of an airport?

WHY IS IT?

People at the airport think it is acceptable to pull out a wedgie where ever it attacks?

WHY IS IT?

I am always seated next to a person who can't afford a handkerchief?

WHY IS IT?

I am always next to a person who sneezes all over the seat in front of them?

WHY IS IT?

So many people wear sun glasses indoors at the airport?

WHY IS IT?

If you ask directions at the airport and they don't know the answer, they will make them up?

WHY IS IT?

People at the airport don't wear matching socks?

WHY IS IT?

A man would wear half socks with little balls on the back of them at the airport?

WHY IS IT?

The husband has to carry three bags and the wife carries her purse?

WHY IS IT?

Its 90 degrees outside and there are people at the airport wearing knit hats?

WHY IS IT?

People dress their kids funny and then take them to the airport?

WHY IS IT?

When you are standing in front of the arrival/departure TV's someone will stop directly in front of you blocking your view?

WHY IS IT?

People carry children in a carrier on their back and then get upset when they throw up on their neck?

WHY IS IT?

People with the worst bodies wear the most revealing clothes?

WHY IS IT?

When you walk into an airport you have a sudden urge to frown?

WHY IS IT?

People will line up to use the pay phone and when it is their turn they will ask you if you have change?

WHY IS IT?

When a sign on the walkway says walk on the left and stand to the right, people will do just the opposite?

WHY IS IT?

When you put on a suit you feel you should get priority treatment?

WHY IS IT?

You carry a laptop computer but you don't have a battery? Status symbol maybe?

WHY IS IT?

Babies don't cry in the airport until they board the plane?

WHY IS IT?

People at the airport will have dark sunglasses on and then try to read a book?

WHY IS IT?

Large women at the airport wear bright colors? Shouldn't they wear camouflage?

WHY IS IT?

The bag the captain carries has an emblem from a world war I fighter group?

WHY IS IT?

People who board the plane under the pretense of needing a little more time seem to get off the plane plenty fast?

WHY IS IT?

I will miss my flight but my bags will make it?

WHY IS IT?

They announce that you can't leave your bags unattended, but when you walk through the gate area you have to climb over unattended bags?

WHY IS IT?

On a regular basis you will see a guy in a suit walking through the seating area looking for an abandoned news paper?

WHY IS IT?

The captain on my aircraft is the one who after walking up one flight of stairs needs 10 minutes to catch his breath?

WHY IS IT?

There is always one passenger who will stop in the isle, set his briefcase down, and sort through his papers?

WHY IS IT?

Passengers will pick a phone that is near the loudest part of the airport and then get mad when they can't hear?

WHY IS IT?

I get stuck next to the woman who takes out a Kleenex and uses it to pick her nose all the time knowing her finger will go through the Kleenex?

WHY IS IT?

A person will wait two hours in the terminal for a flight and still be late boarding the plane?

WHY IS IT?

I get stuck next to an elderly woman who smells like mothballs?

WHY IS IT?

Late arrivals feel it is all right to cram their oversized luggage in the overheads on top of the other peoples luggage?

WHY IS IT?

The airlines request that you be early and then never leave on time?

WHY IS IT?

A passenger will always walk past their seat and then have to turn around against the flow and squeeze through?

WHY IS IT?

I notice these things? Am I the only one who notices?

WHY ME?

I got to the shuttle pick up point just as the shuttle arrived. I got on and found that I was the only passenger. I actually began to think that things were looking up. After three stops I realized that I had rushed to judgment. After the third stop there was one seat left and it was next to me. With one stop to go there was still hope. This hope soon faded. I leaned forward and saw Ma Kettle standing at the last stop and yes she had five bags. Two large bags, one smaller one and two shoulder bags. By this time I am praying that several people will get off at the last stop, but as usual my luck was bad. Ma gets on and spies the seat next to me. She waddles to it not thinking to leave the bags at the front of the shuttle. She stopped next to me and proceeds to drop the two large bags on my left foot. I moaned and jerked my foot free. I began to connect several words together that might be socially unacceptable. This caused her to spin around to see what was happening. As she spun, the bag on her right shoulder smashed into my nose. What came next was unbelievable. As I sat there holding my nose and recoiling in pain she stated, "I am sorry did I hurt you?" I wanted to reach out and pluck out her dentures but I didn't.

33

I just added several words to the string I had started. As if to add insult to injury, ma exited the shuttle before I could. As she stood I covered all major vital areas before she could pick up her bags. She placed the small bags over her shoulders then reached for the large ones. Both shoulder bags dropped and like pendulums they swung toward their targets. I shifted my position causing the first to miss but as I moved to block the second she also moved. It struck me in the sternum driving the air out of my lungs. She must have thought I was from a foreign country because as she left one would swear I was speaking in tongues. I recovered from this experience and proceeded to the gate area. As I passed through the gate I realized that ma was in front of me. I stopped in my tracks and began to shake my head. I felt a hand grip my arm and I heard this voice. I turned toward the voice to see this little old lady. She stated, "Honey don't worry, I fly all the time and trust me it's safe." I thanked her and slipped into the aircraft.

WHY ME?

As usual nothing goes as planned. I decided to change my seat assignment to an emergency aisle because there were only two seats in the row and there was a lot more leg room. At the last moment they changed the type of aircraft to the one where the emergency rows had three seats. I proceeded to my seat only to find that I had twin bouncers on each side of me. I now know how a sardine feels.

WHY ME?

I boarded the plane as the stewardess made her announcements. The last thing she said was that today we had two captains aboard. As I proceeded to my seat I couldn't help but wonder why we needed two? As we left the gate and the pilot hit the brakes we heard a loud squeak. Now I began to worry. Two captains and a creaky old plane, not a good combination. When we took off the plane lurched into the air and when we landed we bounced twice and hit hard. As I left the aircraft I asked the stewardess why we had two captains and she responded that the second captain was in training. Visions of the movie airplane came to mind and I wondered how often I had been on training flights. Shouldn't I get a discount?

WHY ME?

I arrived at the gate and picked a spot to sit way away from the crowd. I watched the other passengers arrive and find a place to sit. As is to be expected, I looked up and here came a man, woman and two little twerps. Where I was sitting there was an aisle that tee's into my row. They didn't sit along the row. No they had to sit at the end of the tee. Each time they moved I had to pull in my feet to allow them to pass. They didn't get up together and pass, no they had to do it one at a time. Eight times they passed and each time I would move. I had enough, I again moved, this time to a corner away from the gate. I didn't have anyone else come close. It must have been the way I looked at people when they came near.

WHY ME?

I am sitting at the gate and I start to notice the condition of other passengers. One elderly man in a sweater and tweed pants had a neck brace on while a young girl in a neon shirt had a broken arm. Three passengers were in wheel chairs and two people were on crutches. I began to wonder, with all the bad luck packed on one flight how long will it be until it effects everyone around them. I attempted to shake the bad feeling so I looked beyond the gate to where I noticed a TV news crew was filming. I walked over to them and found they were filming our flight departure. I began to hope they were not filming to get the early jump on our plane crash.

WHY ME?

I arrive at check in at 0600 for a 0700 flight and no one is there. We hurry to the gate only to find that it is delayed because of fog in Ohio. No one could tell us how long the delay would be for. Two hours later we are still waiting for some word. We change our flight to go through Atlanta and just as we finished we were informed that the fog in Ohio had lifted. They changed our flight back to the original stops and we questioned them about our connections to Vegas. They assured us we would have no problem with connections. We arrived in Ohio in time to see our connection pull off from the gate. I can't count the number of flights that I have been on where they held the flight for late passengers. In my case they will leave early just to piss me off. Now came the hard part. How do we get to Vegas? Instead of 2½ hours it took us 9 hours. We flew from Indianapolis to Ohio, from Ohio to Arizona and then from Arizona to Texas before we arrived in Vegas.

WHY ME?

I was booked on a flight with only 20 people. They had set it up so no one had anyone next to them. Just as they were closing the door I observed a woman squeeze through. This female was wearing low cut tennis shoes, black knee socks, dirty shorts, and a dirty shirt. Her eyes were puffy and her makeup had run making her look like a messenger from hell. I began shaking my head and mumbling "not me again!" I kept shaking my head and hoping against all hope that she passed me by. I was overwhelmed with relief because she passed me by. I laid my head back and closed my eyes as a smile creased my lips. I was jerked back to the present when the female kicked my leg and stated "I need to get by Bub." This messenger from a bad horror movie had walked past her row then realizing her mistake returned to ruin my life. She stepped across my legs and I was over come by the smell of old spice after shave. I wondered why a women would wear a mans after shave but when she crossed her legs I got the answer. She had more hair on her legs than I had on my body. For the next hour she blew her nose and sniffled all the way. Stopping only to shift and clean the nose stud.

WHY ME?

I was on an aircraft on the two seat side when an elderly man entered and sat next to me. I expected the worst but there was no outward symptoms of any problems. I sat there and wondered who would be the distraction for this flight. The stewardess went through her speech and then walked down the aisle.

She stopped at our aisle and turned to the three seat side. There were two men and a women with a 5 month old child. The stewardess informed the mother that there were only three O'2 masks in the overhead dispenser. She then stated that the mother would have to move to the two seat side where there was an extra mask at each row. The guy next to me jumped up and traded places with the mother. As she sat down the baby began to scream. The mother broke off a piece of bagel and placed it into the child's mouth. The kid stopped crying and I took some solace in the fact that it was only a 20 minute flight. I began to smell something strange like an egg, cheese and onion combination. I then heard a "Whew sound" and realized that the kid had gas. I reached up to redirect my air nozzle and heard a gurgling noise. I looked down just in time to see the kid throw up on my leg and shoe. The mother apologized and handed me a wet napkin. I began to clean the nasty smelling stuff off my leg when the mother began to sing to the kid. It was like chalk on a chalk board. Why didn't I bring my CD player. I looked at the child and realized that the child didn't like the singing either. He screwed up his face and began to scream. The only positive thing I could see was that the kid was making his mother miserable also.

WHY IS IT?

The captain comes on the PA and announces that there has been a change. The people who were supposed to stay on this aircraft for the final leg of the flight will have to change planes because of problems with this aircraft. The announcement comes half way through the flight. Why can't they wait to warn us until we are on the ground?

WHY IS IT?

I get stuck next to a person who smacks their lips the whole trip?

WHY ME?

I was sitting on the aircraft when I observed a subject enter. He was wearing tan pants, a torn tee shirt, red sweat shirt, blue jacket, and glasses that made his eyes look huge. This guy had greasy hair parted down the middle. I probably would not have noticed him except for the fact that it was 90 degrees outside and he was dressed for winter. He dropped down next to me and crossed his left foot over his right leg. From the moment he sat down until the end of the flight, he had an unnatural twitching of both legs. I couldn't help but wonder which loony bin he had escaped from. I kept looking at him knowing I had seen him before. About 10 minutes into the flight I realized where I knew him from. He was the double for the actor who played D. B. Cooper the first airplane high-jacker. The rest of the flight I sat there waiting for him to make his move. I didn't know what I was going to do but I was ready.

WHY ME?

While waiting to board my plane I observed four adults walk up with five babies. I wondered what they had put in the water here. With my luck I figured they all would be seated near me. Finally my row was called and as I entered the plane I was greeted by a stewardess who looked like the wicked witch of the north. I wanted to ask how she got out from under the house. I took my seat which was located next to a spiffy dresser. He had a striped shirt, checkered pants, and light gray socks with a yellow strip around them. I thought that this guy was lucky he was going to Florida because only in Florida would he fit in. During the $1^3/_4$ hour trip this guy picked his nose 9 times. He would use his right hand to pick it and wipe it on his left shoulder. I was glad I was on his right side.

WHY ME?

We received a page and were informed that if we didn't get to the airport right away we would be stuck for the night. This was due to severe weather. We raced to the airport and proceeded to miss our exit. It cost me about ten minutes. I arrived at the airport , grabbed my bags, and ran into the lobby. I ran up to check in and was then informed that if I had been there just five minutes earlier I would have made the earlier flight. I begged her to call the gate and I found the plane was still there. I ran through the airport , bags in hand to the gate. They had to bang on the side of the aircraft to get them to open the door. I got on the plane and went to the last row where my seat assignment was. The pilot began to start the engines which were located over my shoulder. I immediately went deaf in my left ear and after about an hour I figure I wouldn't be able to have kids. When I got home I found the weather scare was canceled and I realized that I didn't have to go through this journey from hell after all.

WHY ME?

I was sitting in my assigned seat when I noticed a female heading my way. She was a bleached blond with a hair cut like Mo of the three stooges. She was heading for the bathroom and as she got closer I realized that she put her make up on with a shovel. She had shaved the hair off the back of her head and you would think this was enough of an attention getter but not for her. She also had a red, blue and brown tattoo that covered the back of her head. I began to pray that none of my sons would ever bring a woman like this home to meet his parents.

WHY ME?

While in flight we ran into some rain. Just as we came out of it I noticed a wide range of colors reflecting off the clouds. I soon realized that it was a rainbow which completely circled the aircraft like a doughnut. I began to laugh when I thought back to my Bible class days. We were taught that the rainbow was given as a promise not to ever flood the world again. If instead of the rainbow we were given the doughnut it could have been a completely different story.

WHY IS IT?

They tell you to be prepared for heightened security and it consists of a person at check in asking you if anyone had you carry a package on?

WHY IS IT?

The speaker system on the aircraft has no medium? It's either too loud or too soft!

WHY IS IT?

There are never any places to put your briefcase on so everyone gets down on their knees and uses the floor!

WHY IS IT?

People wear their hat backwards at the airport? I guess they don't know if their coming or going!

WHY IS IT?

People plan to arrive late so they can run to the gate? Are they health nuts or idiots?

WHY IS IT?

Some people at the airport will walk one way while facing the other?

WHY IS IT?

These people are shocked when they run into something?

WHY IS IT?

People wear their glasses on top of their head? Is their prescription too strong?

WHY IS IT?

Blue hair seems to glow at the airport?

WHY IS IT?

Women with a body that should be hidden, cover it with terry cloth so it will stick to all the wrong places?

WHY IS IT?

The terry cloth is always purple?

WHY IS IT?

Some people will wear ugly shoes and then stand like Charlie Chaplin with their toes out to draw attention to them?

WHY IS IT?

People at airports wear clothes that identify them as athletes?

WHY IS IT?

Most of these people wearing athlete clothes have never been athletes?

WHY IS IT?

So many women at the airport have long nose hairs?

WHY IS IT?

There are so many nicks and dents in the aircraft I fly?

WHY IS IT?

I never see them until I off load?

WHY IS IT?

The colors used at the airport are so ugly?

WHY IS IT?

The guy in front of me can't sit still?

WHY IS IT?

Manufacturers can't make luggage that airlines can't poke holes in?

WHY IS IT?

Manufacturers don't use bullet proof vest material in luggage?

WHY IS IT?

Mr. machismo will never be seen doing anything uncool but he will be at the gate with balloons and candy?

WHY ME?

I arrived at the airport early and rode the shuttle from the long term parking lot. By the second stop most of the people had exited the shuttle. I rode to the terminal in unexpected comfort. I checked in and got a sandwich with no problems at all. I began to wonder where the problems would begin and how bad they would be. I arrived at the gate and verified that it was the correct one for my flight then I went to use the phone. When I returned I discovered that they had delayed my flight. This wouldn't be bad in normal circumstances but the delay would cause me to arrive two minutes after my connection was scheduled to depart. I asked what the situation was in Chicago. They asked me if I wanted to leave the next day. I informed them that was not possible. They just shrugged their shoulders. I asked what terminal was my flight going into and they said "C." I asked what terminal the departing connection was listed to. They said " B." I asked if there was a chance I could make it and she said "Doubt It." I decided to chance it. I arrived in Chicago and rushed to the assigned gate on "B" concourse. I was informed that the gate mechanism was malfunctioning. They told me that the flight was rerouted to the "C" concourse. I ran for the gate hoping that they would be there. I reached the gate just as they were preparing to leave. I then sat there for 25 minutes waiting for them to decide which of the four people assigned to 12 B was going to go on the flight. We taxied and I noticed that the guy next to me kept pinching a zit on his chin. For the next 20 minutes I watched him pinch his zit then look at his fingers. He did this thirteen times in the 20 minutes. He stopped when they came around with the drinks and I thought I had a reprieve. After he finished he began to mess with his right foot. He removed his slipper and began to scratch. To my surprise, as he scratched the bottom of his foot chunk after chunk of dead meat flaked off. I needed to get my mind off him so I pulled out my computer and began the ritual of turning it on and getting ready to work. During the wait I dropped the mouse two times. Mr. foot scratcher stated that he could see my mouse took a beating. I felt like adding him to the list. I survived the flight and arrived at the hotel. The bad feeling was back. I was met with a sign, "Lobby Closed Use Drive Up Window." We beat on the window and an elderly man appeared. He waved us back to the lobby and let us in. We began to have a discussion with him and then discovered that he was legally deaf. He took our credit card and after 15 minutes of trying to scan it backward he finally turned it around and it was accepted. I got to my room totally exhausted at 1 AM knowing that I had to be up at 0530. I had the sudden urge to relieve my self and after a successful completion I found that the flush handle didn't work. I was forced to clear off the back of the toilet lift the lid, and reach my arm in to manually flush it. I picked up the phone and called the desk. No one answered. The next morning I again called the desk and again no one answered. We tried to locate a manager and were told that was not possible. I left shaking my head.

WHY IS IT?

People buy bite size cookies then take three bites to eat each one of them?

WHY IS IT?

Skinny people eat low fat food?

WHY IS IT?

I checked into the hotel and settled in for a well deserved rest. At midnight another subject entered my room. We had a heart to heart talk only to discover that they had rented my room twice.

WHY IS IT?

I am always next to a guy that eats so loud that you want to choke him?

WHY IS IT?

Mental midgets always search me out and want to talk to me?

WHY IS IT?

I have to fly from Cleveland to Chicago to get to Indianapolis?

WHY IS IT?

There are never any direct flights?

WHY IS IT?

I always get in the line that goes no where?

WHY IS IT?

The food you order at the airport never looks as good as the picture at the restaurant?

WHY IS IT?

Airline slogans are seldom true? Friendly skies? How can they be friendly when you never leave on time?

WHY IS IT?

It's not the sky that needs to be friendly it's the time you spend on the ground that kills me?

WHY IS IT?

They always seem to have the same excuse for late planes?

WHY IS IT?

Your car works fine until you get ready to go to the airport?

WHY IS IT?

Perfectly normal people trip when walking on flat surfaces at the airport.

WHY IS IT?

They don't have lockers to lock small kids in at the airport?

WHY IS IT?

People working at security check points protecting my life look like they wasted theirs?

WHY IS IT?

Airports use mental midgets to design their curb pick up for new arrivals?

WHY IS IT?

All the lost people end up driving around the airport?

WHY IS IT?

It takes longer to get out of the parking lot than it takes to drive across the state?

WHY IS IT?

There are 15 toll gates out of the parking lot but only one is open?

WHY IS IT?

When I have exact change, there are never any exact change gates?

WHY IS IT?

The stewardess used to look ladylike, but now they look like they beat up people for a living?

WHY IS IT?

The person who picks me up from my flight waits 1 hour for my arrival then 20 minutes into the drive home they have to stop to go pee?

WHY IS IT?

When we stop for him to go pee and I stay in the van he turns on the alarm so I can't get out?

WHY IS IT?

When the door is opened the alarm can't be shut off without the key?

WHY IS IT?

He took the key with him?

WHY ME?

I requested an emergency row with two seats so I could have plenty of room and I could get some sleep. This plane had a three seat side but at the exit there were only two seats and a space next to the door. A woman and her husband seated themselves behind me and soon I could hear him snoring. I ignored the noise and drifted off to sleep. To my surprise the wife tapped me on the shoulder on the emergency door side. I woke with a start and found her bent over and asking for me to let her out my row. She stated that she didn't want to wake her husband up so she used my row. For a moment I considered pulling the emergency door lever and dropping her like a rock but instead I stood and let her out. I went back to sleep and here she was again. With venom in my eyes I let her in and decided what move I should make next. I waited for about 10 minutes until they were both deep in sleep. Then I made my move. I went around the end seat by the door as she had done. I shook both of them as she had done me and asked to pass. Before they could move, I excused my self and squeezed through making sure I stepped on each and every foot I could. He began to mumble as I passed. I leaned down and got within two inches of his face and stated "Talk to your wife." When I returned they avoided my gaze and when the plane landed they went past me in a hurry.

WHY ME?

I boarded the aircraft and found that I had an aisle seat so I knew I was going to get the heck beat out of me by passing passengers. After being banged by the first 20 passengers my attention was diverted to the guy sitting across the aisle from me. I noticed that his eyes were blinking extremely fast as if a heart attack was occurring. I began to think that it was just my luck that this guy would fall out, need CPR and mouth to mouth and I would be the only one trained to do it. Looking a little closer I noticed the guy was also twitching on a regular basis. He twitched his head from side to side and then up and down. I observed the mannerisms for about fifteen minutes and realized that he was also reading a magazine upside down. I couldn't take it anymore, I got up and went to the stewardess. I looked at her and asked her if I could "TWITCH" my seat. She looked at me quizzically then said, Oh your seated next to the guy with the twitch. I laughed uncontrollably as she reseated me.

WHY IS IT?

People sucking on hard candy will search me out to smack their lips around me?

WHY IS IT?

The switches for the head phones on the plane are not located where you can get to them with out hitting the person next to you?

WHY IS IT?

My seat will never lay back?

WHY IS IT?

They can serve a 2″ square piece of bread and call it a sandwich?

WHY IS IT?

People wait to cough uncontrollably until the plane takes off?

WHY IS IT?

You have to secure your bag but you can have a baby on your lap for take off?

WHY IS IT?

I get stuck next to a mother and child in the same seat?

WHY IS IT?

I get stuck next to a mother with twin screaming kids?

WHY IS IT?

On a short flight they still serve drinks?

WHY IS IT?

When ever I use the bathroom at the airport, the urinal will flush before I can walk away?

WHY IS IT?

The urinals always have water pressure that is too high?

WHY IS IT?

The water sprays the front of my pants making it look like I had an accident?

WHY ME?

I had to teach a two day class in Arizona and I arrived at the airport there was a blinding rain storm. I recovered my bags and met my transportation. We drove off into the desert and after all signs of life faded away I asked "Where Is It We Are Going?" I was met with evasive comments. The driver began to talk about how rattle snakes would slither under doors and strike the occupants when they got out of bed in the mornings. I took little notice of the conversation. The driver began to tell how snakes would get close to humans to share their warmth. I began to question the folly with which I had agreed to teach in the desert. In the distance I could pick out a single light. As we approached I made the comment that it looked like an old abandon army base. The driver looked at me and said "Air Base" then turned away. Just my luck. I was thrown back to basic training as we passed the huts that housed troops in the past. We pulled up to several single story huts with metal roofs. No lights could be seen but when the lightning flashed I got the impression that I was entering the set of a "B" movie. I got my bags and watched each step for rattlers. We stopped in front of an unmarked door and the driver handed me a key. I opened the door and found the hotel room from hell . I turned on the light and the harsh light exposed the worst decorated room I had ever seen. The chairs and couch were below bean bag quality It appeared to be pre WWII vintage. The carpet was brownish yellow and it had paths warn in it from previous occupants. I stumbled in and dropped my bags as I sat in the chair. I discovered that there wasn't enough pad to keep my but off the board frame. I got up and went into the kitchen for a drink of water and discovered that there was a note posted. It stated that no child less than one year old should drink the water. It further stated that the water contained contaminants from agricultural by-products. In small letters it stated that adults shouldn't fear drinking it. I hesitated, looked at the glass of water, then dumped it and proceeded to the bedroom to discover what other interesting things I might find. Immediately I noticed the bedroom door was a louver door with a gap under it. I began to replay the drivers conversation in my head and abruptly I turned toward the front door. As I expected there was a two inch gap under the front door also. Worrying about snakes, I slowly walked into the bedroom. I had to turn on three lamps to find one with a good bulb. I searched the room for snakes and then moved the night stand close to the bed so I could turn on the light with out stepping to the floor. The beds were sway backs and the shower had green moss growing on the walls. The bathroom window had a small rug over it as a blind. I decided to call home and describe my trip to hell and have my wife write it down for a future book. I picked up the phone and was immediately transported back to the time of Alexander Graham Bell. The phone echoed and hissed and I could hear faint voices in the distance. I turned over the phone and found a sticker dating back to 1933. As suspected, I was not able to complete the call. I went to bed worrying about snakes, wondering what would happen next and why me!!

WHY ME?

I asked for an exit row window seat on my flight to Vegas but there were none left. The clerk recommended that I take a seat toward the front which was an isle seat. She stated that I would like the seat she had assigned me. The aircraft I boarded was a wide body with two rows of three seats on the outside and a larger center row. I was in the three seat side on the isle when a husband and wife combo entered and sat next to me. The pair were like mutt and Jeff. The man was 5'8" tall and 120 pounds where the woman was 5'6" and 305 pounds. The husband sat next to me and the wife took the window seat. It appeared that the husband didn't want to crowd the wife so he began to lean into me. I adjusted by leaning into the aisle. During the flight they served sack lunches and the wife got three of them. During her meal she ordered two mixed drinks and a coke. When she completed the meal she asked the husband to rub her back. He squirmed around and began the task. She moaned and groaned for a while and then with out warning she flopped back pinning her husband to the seat. He squirmed for a minute but before any major damage was done he freed himself. I leaned back and soon fell asleep. I began to dream I was on a boat in the ocean and the wind was just screaming. I abruptly woke up and discovered that what I had heard was the wife snoring extremely loud. I looked around and found that most passengers were visibly upset because her snoring was interrupting the in flight movie. The funny thing was everyone had head phones on and they still could hear the snoring. I settled back in my seat determined to not let it bother me when I noticed that the wife had shifted in her seat. The movement was like she lifted one cheek then the other. I let it pass until my eyes started to water. I looked at the husband and noticed that he had placed his handkerchief over his nose. I took out my handkerchief and placed two mints in it and then placed it over my nose. This only made the rotten smell be minty bad. I heard the clatter rise as the cloud passed from row to row. The husband was over come and leaned forward and placed his face in his hand. This provided me the opportunity to let those affected know where it had come from. I extended my arm and pointed at her as I turned on my overhead light. I heard comments like "Who Stabbed The Cat? and "Someone Light A Match Quick." One affected passenger requested that she step outside. Maybe they need to announce no smoking or any form of air pollution is allowed during the flight.

WHY IS IT?

No one at the hotel speaks English?

WHY IS IT?

No one at the hotel has a clue as to what is going on?

WHY IS IT?

The phone in my room is so far away from my bed?

WHY IS IT?

They then advertise a wake up call?

WHY IS IT?

They bolt the TV remote to a table that is so far from the bed that you have to get up to use it? Is that where they get the term "remote?"

WHY IS IT?

The toilet paper is always mounted where it is impossible to get to?

WHY IS IT?

Moss grows on a different side of a shower than a tree?

WHY IS IT?

I always have to change the roll of paper in the bathroom?

WHY IS IT?

When it's hot I have a heater that works? When it's cold I have an air conditioner that works?

WHY IS IT?

The massage head in the shower never has enough pressure to massage?

WHY IS IT?

When you ask a question at the desk, they act like you are not there?

WHY IS IT?

Most employees at hotels are goofy? There must be a training course for this. it can't be coincidence. They need to look for a new gene pool!!!

WHY IS IT?

I check in a hotel, carry my 200 pound bag in only to find my room is on the third floor and there is no elevator?

WHY IS IT?

I get to the room and find the directions for the phone are hand written?

WHY IS IT?

It's 90 degrees outside and the only light in the bathroom is a heat lamp?

WHY IS IT?

This same hotel had window locks but none of them worked?

WHY IS IT?

There are three squares of toilet paper on the roll and they don't put a new roll on?

WHY IS IT?

They use toilet paper made out of tree bark?

WHY IS IT?

I always get stuck next to a guy who is allergic to soap and water?

WHY IS IT?

I have to stand next to him on a shuttle and he grabs a strap so his arm pit is in my face?

WHY IS IT?

They have a box to measure the size of bags but not people? Have you ever seen someone get stuck in an aircraft bathroom? I have!!

WHY IS IT?

When the seat belt sign comes on and they announce that every one should stay in their seat, there is a mad rush for the bathroom?

WHY IS IT?

The only people who have to go to the bathroom are the ones who sit in the window seat?

WHY IS IT?

If you sit in the exit row the people behind you always kick the back of your seat? Don't they know it's not smart to piss off the guy in the exit seat?

WHY IS IT?

When you check in at the airport they say you owe $193, and when you pay cash they don't know what to do?

WHY IS IT?

When you give them cash they tell you they don't have anyway to change a twenty?

WHY IS IT?

In the pre-flight briefing they talk about everything except the bathroom? Since people wait till they get on the plane to go potty, they should announce "you people who waited till the last minute so you could delay the flight, now is the time to go." For fun give bats to the passengers so they can demonstrate their displeasure as they walk by!

WHY IS IT?

Some people will change dirty diapers in their chairs and not in the bathroom?

WHY IS IT?

Some people go to the bathroom, don't lock the door, and then get upset when someone opens the door on them?

WHY IS IT?

Some parents will take their child to the bathroom and hold the door open on them?

WHY IS IT?

This same parent can't understand that a little boy can't pee when a whole plane full of people are watching his performance?

WHY IS IT?

People can't read the most fundamental words in society like "Occupied?"

WHY IS IT?

When they see the word occupied, they try the door and see if it is locked? Then as if to doubt themselves, they knock and ask "is anyone in there."

WHY IS IT?

People line up in a plane to go to the bathroom?

WHY IS IT?

I have to be next to a guy who snarf's after each bite of dinner?

WHY IS IT?

He sits next to me and not his wife?

WHY IS IT?

The bathroom is so close to the exits? Could it have a duel meaning? Exit & Evacuate?

DAAAAAA?

A women walked up to the stewardess after looking into both bathrooms. She asked if one was for men and one for women??????????

WHY ME?

Terry was stuck in front of a child who came on the flight with a small car. The child kept driving the car around the top of seat terry was seated in. This would not be to bad except that every third lap the kid would roll the car over and around Terry's head. Terry turned to the kid's mother and asked for her assistance. She put down her news paper and said the child's name and counted to three. Before she reached three the kid would stop. The mother would go back to her news paper and the kid would begin again. As red marks began to appear on Terry's bald spot he again appealed to the mother. As before she stated the kids name and counted. Terry wished she would count fast and then knock the shit out of the kid but that was not in the cards. As before the kid stopped until she began to read . For the next thirty minutes each time on the kids third lap Terry would convulsively lean forward to avoid new injuries. After they landed Terry turned to the mother and thanked her. She asked him why he was thanking her. Terry stood over her and the kid and stated that before this flight he was undecided on the issue of abortion but now he knew there was a time and a place for abortion.

WHY ME?

I checked into the hotel and did my normal screening expecting to find every thing wrong. I checked the bed, bathroom, windows, and chairs. To my amazement everything was right in the world. I hung up my cloths and settled in for a short nap. I was awakened by severe cramping. I ran to the bathroom before nature could call. My only goal was to relieve the pain in my stomach. As I prepared to do my business something extremely cold struck me on the bare back. My sphincter slammed shut and the pain intensified. I shook off the effect of the cold and was again ready to relieve the pain when as before something extremely cold struck me between the shoulder blades. As before the sphincter slammed shut and I almost doubled over in pain. I looked above my head searching for the cause of the torturer only to find that there was a leak directly over my head. Before I died I had to do something to stop the delay. I grabbed a towel and threw it over me so I could finish. When I recovered I went looking for a manager. It was determined that the leak was coming from an ice machine on the next floor.

WHY ME?

I flew into Alabama and checked into my room only to find that the air-conditioning didn't work. I checked with the desk and they assured they would have someone look at it the next day. I went to the lecture room and found that it was extremely hot there also. I again contacted the desk and they assured me that it would be taken care of. I suffered through the first night with no air and when I went to the lecture room I had high expectations. I found that it was even hotter there. I began to lecture only to find that the rain that fell during the night had backed up in the lecture room. As I walked across the floor you could hear the sloshing echoing from wall to wall. I demanded another room but none was available. I delayed the lecture long enough for them to come in and vacuum up some of the water. Things seemed to work well until I turned on the overhead projector. I got the shock of my life. In fact I came so close to fouling my pants it was unreal. I stepped away from the machine and noticed that there was a slight smoke coming off the hair on my arms. I called the desk and their response was to bring me a large rubber mat for me to stand on. I resumed the lecture and things were going well until the ceilings tiles began to fall. The first one knocked the pointer out of my hand. This was enough for me to give the class a break. I went outside and lowered the flag to half staff in anticipation of morning for the staff if they didn't do something about my miserable experiences at their hotel. I then went hunting for the staff.

WHY IS IT?

When ever I order a sandwich at a hotel they burn one side?

WHY IS IT?

They place the burnt side down on the plate?

WHY IS IT?

When you order a salad at the hotel it looks like they used yard clippings?

WHY IS IT?

My hotel door always has a gap under it?

WHY IS IT?

My hotel door always faces into the wind?

WHY IS IT?

The TV is always located just out of view when you are in the bathroom?

WHY IS IT?

My hotel room is under some one with a peg leg?

WHY IS IT?

Their room is small but they never stop walking around?

WHY IS IT?

I am always next to some one who reads books from the back to the front?

WHY IS IT?

The person behind me never covers their mouth when they cough up part of their lung?

WHY IS IT?

I always get the stewardess that has to wear a bag with a draw string?

WHY IS IT?

When it is freezing cold, some goof will pack his clothes in 5 small suitcases instead of one large one?

WHY IS IT?

This same guy will flag down the parking lot shuttle and hold the door open to load the bags one at a time?

WHY IS IT?

When this happens I am the one closest to the door and farthest from the heater?

WHY IS IT?

My wife can never find toilet paper in the women's bathroom? What do they do with it?

DAAAAAA?

I sat behind a women going to Vegas who had a few bricks short of a full load. When directions were given as to how to fasten our seat belts she needed help from the stewardess to accomplish the task. Once we reached cruising altitude she buzzed the stewardess so she could explain how to recline her seat. The stewardess had to show her twice. Once she accomplished this task she must have been worn out because she fell asleep and began to snore extremely loud. This is when I noticed that she had two huge warts on her nose. About this time my wife made an astute observation. She noted that this woman couldn't work the seat belt but she was in an emergency row and if we crashed she would probably ask how to open the emergency exit.

WHY IS IT?

I have to leave two hours early to get to the airport on time?

WHY IS IT?

If I am running late, I get behind some farmer who has never seen a modern highway?

WHY IS IT?

This farmer has a speedometer that only goes up to 45 miles per hour?

WHY IS IT?

When I am running late I will always come up on an accident just before I get to the airport? At least this way I can see my plane leave.

WHY IS IT?

When I am running late, every traffic light on the way to the airport will be red?

WHY IS IT?

When I am running late, one of the lights will be stuck on red for my direction?

WHY IS IT?

When I am running late and the light is stuck, there is always a police officer there so you can't run the light?

WHY IS IT?

When I am running late and an officer is directing traffic at the light that is stuck, he will always let traffic go until I get to the front then stop me?

WHY IS IT?

When I am running late, the long term parking lot is full and I have to park in the over flow lot?

WHY IS IT?

The overflow lot is always 20 miles from the airport?

WHY IS IT?

The shuttle for the overflow lot only comes around on even hours?

WHY IS IT?

The shuttle drivers need passes from the work release center?

WHY IS IT?

I always get a driver that forgets the route so you pass the airport twice before you off load?

WHY IS IT?

When I get to the shuttle pick up point, the shuttle is always pulling away?

WHY IS IT?

The only time the shuttle driver smiles is when he is pulling away from you?

WHY IS IT?

The airport will change shuttle pick up points and not tell any one?

WHY IS IT?

When you ask where the new pick up points are, they look at you like your stupid?

WHY IS IT?

They put the vital information, like entrances and exits on small signs with little writing?

WHY IS IT?

They welcome you at each airport? In most cases, if you did not have to be there you wouldn't be.

WHY IS IT?

They don't post the crime stat's for the city at the airport?

WHY IS IT?

You search out the farthest corner of the airport to sleep and some loud mouth will sit next to you and carry on a conversation with an imaginary friend?

WHY IS IT?

It's 1 degree at the airport when you arrive and someone will be there in shorts and a tee shirt?

WHY IS IT?

No matter where I sit, someone will pull out finger nail polish and do their nails? Most times it's so strong I forget what day it is?

WHY IS IT?

When I return from a trip and go to the long term parking lot to get my car, I find they piled snow behind it and I can't get out?

WHY IS IT?

My luggage never arrives at the airport when I do?

WHY IS IT?

When I get in line to fill out a claim form, the woman in front of me takes 30 minutes?

WHY IS IT?

After my flight arrives they close the airport?

WHY IS IT?

There are never any taxis when you need them?

WHY IS IT?

The hotels I stay in never provide shuttle service?

WHY IS IT?

The only time I don't have a problem traveling is when I have all the time in the world?

WHY IS IT?

When I check in, the only airline that is busy is mine?

WHY IS IT?

There is never anyone at the express check in?

WHY IS IT?

There are 100 people in line and only three people to wait on us?

WHY ME?

There are only three seats left on the plane one of which is next to me. Three people arrive. A father, a mother, and a small child. Why is it the child is placed next to me? Why is it, the child wants to hold a two hour conversation and she refuses to stop talking to me unless I sing her to sleep?

WHY IS IT?

People don't mark their luggage so they can identify them? Do they really like to pick up every bag on the conveyer in order to find theirs?

WHY IS IT?

Some airports use the modern concept for seating? They arrange an area that will seat 100 so it will only seat 15?

WHY IS IT?

I leave winter behind to go to Florida only to find a cold front waiting for me?

WHY IS IT?

It warms up when I leave and gets worst when I get home?

WHY IS IT?

There is a train yard next to the hotel and every hour on the hour they greet each other by blowing their horn?

WHY IS IT?

Jet fighters have to scramble over my hotel room at 11:58 PM?

WHY IS IT?

So many airline support vehicles are wrecked? If they wreck their little vehicles one would think they would wreck their big vehicles. What qualifications are required to drain airline toilets?

WHY IS IT?

So many people at airports wear plaids? In combinations?

WHY IS IT?

Everyone wants to talk to me when I am trying to sleep?

WHY IS IT?

People wear hiking boots to the airport? Do they know the airlines intend to send them over a mountain to their next connection?

WHY IS IT?

People wear spiked dog collars around their neck at the airport?

WHY IS IT?

They don't have professional referees at places where lines form at the airport?

WHY IS IT?

People wear their pants below their hips so it looks like they have short legs and long bodies?

WHY IS IT?

When a person cuts in line and is confronted they act indignant?

WHY IS IT?

It seems like parents use the airport as a cheap baby-sitter?

WHY IS IT?

You see a marked police car on the runway with a plane? Are they stopping it for speeding?

WHY ME?

I am flying into St. Louis and the pilot lands the aircraft with a hard bump. He came on the PA and stated the landing was not the best but look at the bright side , we made it! The stewardess came on and stated that we should be careful when we open the overheads because on this flight there was no doubt the bags had shifted!

WHY IS IT?

I am always on the plane that drips water on me from the over head?

WHY IS IT?

I get stuck behind three kids with hot little cars and they drive them over their seat and mine?

WHY IS IT?

They seem to always need to work on my plane at the gate? What does it mean when they jack the plane up and begin to lower and raise the landing gear? What does it mean when a guy has to pour large cans of oil in the jet engines of my plane?

WHY IS IT?

Seasoned citizens seem to search me out to cough on me?

WHY IS IT?

When I hurry through the airport to my gate they always delay the flight?

WHAT DOES IT MEAN WHEN?

The stewardess states, "as soon as we get the thumbs up, we will board you."

WHY ME?

I was taking a shuttle to the airport in Dallas and I was surprised that they sent two drivers. they were two blond females and they began to have a conversation about current events. I was in the back and I noticed that the more they talked the faster she drove. We soon reached 75 miles per hour and I started to fidget a little. I noticed that there was a pick up truck in front of us and there was a strange lean to their roll bar. All of a sudden the roll bar fell off and slid across the highway. The shuttle driver reacted like a defensive driving instructor and proceeded to avoid the roll bar by running two cars off the road. By this time my butt had a grip on the seat that was even better than the seat belt. The shuttle driver received several long blasts from horns and one could hear some animated language being used. The shuttle driver was incensed that someone had the audacity to honk at her. She retaliated with a string of adjectives and descriptive nouns before realizing where she was at. She glanced in the mirror and caught my eye and apologized stating she was sorry but she used to be a cab driver. After a few moments of silence she again addressed me. She stated "This isn't going to effect my tip is it?" I said nothing.

WHY ME?

I was giving a class in Vegas at a noted hotel. The room was packed and I was on a roll. As I got into the lecture I noticed that one person in the front row began to sway back and forth. I continued on and found that this guy leaned over and slid out of his chair and onto all fours under the table. I've been a lecturer for many years and I normally can tune out most distraction that occur but in this case the subject began to throw up on the floor under the table. The show must go on so I continued and attempted to ignore the heavier as I walked to the opposite side of the room. This guy must have had a stomach the size of a wash tub because he kept going and going and going. After about 5 minutes of this everyone in the room was watching him and not me. So I stated that since it was obvious that he wasn't going to take a break then we might as well. There was a quick exodus and the clean up crew was requested.

WHY IS IT?

I check in a hotel only to find that I get no hot water for three days?

WHY IS IT?

I have to share my room with bugs that can't be described?

WHY IS IT?

I get stuck next to someone who has to read out loud to understand the story?

WHY IS IT?

When the elevator is out at the airport the escalator is out also?

WHY IS IT?

The 13th floor is listed as the 14th? I am not sure I like the reason!

WHY IS IT?

When I try to sleep at the airport someone will plop down right next to me driving the seat into my head?

WHY IS IT?

I get stuck next to a group that tell stupid jokes that no one laughs at?

WHY IS IT?

The constitution guarantees free speech except when you tell an airline employee that the way they treated you was shitty? Can they say I can't say shitty to them at the airport? Is the airport a constitutionally exempt location? I guess it is!

WHY IS IT?

You can hear airport employees using every kind of cuss word at the airport, but I can't say shitty? I think that is a pretty shitty deal!!!

WHY ME?

I was going to Gulfport Mississippi by way of Atlanta. When I arrived in Atlanta I was advised that my connecting flight was being delayed. I sat down and began to wait. After a while a female employee walked up to the gate and I asked her why the plane was late. She stated they didn't have a plane. I asked her was it due to mechanical problems? She said "no." I asked her if it was due to weather? She said "no." I then asked what else is there to cause the delay? She looked at me and said, "I told you we don't have any planes!" Question: Why book passengers if you don't have any planes!!!!!

WHY IS IT?

The airline cancels three flights because there were not enough passengers. When the passengers get mad they make the following announcement, "If you are angry with employees you will be escorted from the airport!"

WHY ME?

I was stuck flying turbo props out of Atlanta when I was notified that we did not have a plane to fly out on. This kind of disturbed me so I began questioning an employee and found out that not only did they not have a plane for my flight they were short 5 planes total. My flight was to leave at 8:20 PM so I settled in for a wait. 9:20 PM arrived and went. 10:30 PM arrived and went with the only change was they were now short 6 aircraft. I began to wonder how an airline could book 6 different flights and then not have any planes show up at the gate. I could understand if it was weather but the employee assured me it was not. I began to worry that I may have to sleep on the floor when they announced a gate change for my flight. My excitement diminished when I got to the new gate and they informed me it was in error. I returned to the original gate and found that several other passengers were in the same predicament. After several minutes they again announced a gate change for me. I hurried to the new gate only to be told that it had changed again. This is when it hit me. They were sending all the passengers from the 6 missing flights to different areas of the airport. I guess they felt that if they separated the masses there was a lower chance of rebellion.

WHY IS IT?

I get stuck behind a women who has extremely stiff hair 3 foot long?

WHY IS IT?

She has to flip it over the back of her seat so it is sticking two inches from my face?

WHY IS IT?

She has to use a goo on it that makes my nose run and my eyes water?

WHY IS IT?

When I ask about getting on the standby list, the guy at the counter says he only does luggage?

WHY IS IT?

When he said that, the girl looked at me and said "he's just labor." Well what the heck is she?

WHY IS IT?

When a guy has three seats in a row by himself, he will lift the arms and lay with his stinky bare feet next to me?

WHY IS IT?

They explain that before you open an emergency exit look for fire outside? Why don't they tell you what to do then? Do you stay inside and cook?

WHY IS IT?

The women next to me not only takes off her shoes, but she has to crack each and every toe knuckle? I never thought of it before, do your toes have knuckles?

WHY IS IT?

Passengers wear suspenders so tight that their butt is at their neck?

WHY IS IT?

I am always behind someone who has dandruff as big as baseballs?

WHY IS IT?

I get stuck next to someone who looks like my third grade teacher?

WHY IS IT?

There is no law limiting the number of times that a person can lean over you to get in the overhead?

WHY IS IT?

There is no law limiting the number of times a person can climb over you to go to the bathroom?

WHY IS IT?

There is no law requiring a person to notify passengers when they pass gas?

WHY IS IT?

There is no law that when a seat starts to show salt rings it must be cleaned?

WHY IS IT?

Airlines don't tell you that your flight is canceled until they delay it 5 times over 4 hours?

WHY IS IT?

When a boy is 10 or older, his mother still accompanies him to the bathroom?

WHY IS IT?

The airlines use spotted carpet? Is it to hide the spills?

WHY IS IT?

The this airlines use urine color seat covers?

WHY ME?

I was picked up at the airport by an employee for the company who's job it was to transport me to the hotel. As we drove he proceeded to reach over in front of me to retrieve a cup that was in a cup holder. He would then spit tobacco juice into the cup and then replace it. I began wondering why he didn't use the holder closer to him instead of grossing me out with the cup of brown swill. This action continued for some time and I began to get more and more uncomfortable with the scenario. As we got closer to the hotel he reached for the cup and it slipped out of his hand. To my horror I watch the brown swill cascade down toward my left leg. It struck me just above the knee and then soaked the pants to my ankle. I could feel it penetrate the pant leg and then run down my leg to where my sock began to soak it up like a little dam. My stomach began to spin as I responded to the physiological impact of the situation. In the nick of time I saw the hotel come into view and I made a bee line bags and baggage for my room. I dumped them on the floor and stripped the affected clothes off and began to shower the offending liquid off till I bled. All the time I was scrubbing I wondered why this has to happen to me!!

WHY IS IT?

Parents will let their kids punch all the buttons overhead on the aircraft?

WHY IS IT?

They show the emergency door placed in the seat on their emergency card knowing full well if the crap hits the fan the seat will be thrown a hundred yards from the plane?

WHY IS IT?

When they give their water landing speech they say don't exit the rear cone of the plane? Don't they think we will notice it is under water?

WHY IS IT?

There is no law that says someone at the hotel has to speak English?

WHY IS IT?

The guy in front of me picks his nose then rubs his lips with his fingers? The guy then eats one bag of peanuts and two cookies with the bugger picken hand.

WHY IS IT?

They seem to sell my seat to more than one passenger on the same flight?

WHY ME?

I checked into a well known hotel only to find that after a few minutes of walking around in my socks they turned black. I noticed that there was a wet spot on the ceiling and mold had started to grow. It was a pretty green so I decided I was too tired to argue about it and move to a new room. I settled in for the night and drifted off to sleep only to awaken to loud laughter and thuds against the outside of the building. I went to the sliding door and found that a baseball team was playing a pick up game in the parking lot. I looked at the clock and noted that it was 9 PM. I went back to bed. I was again awakened to the sound of doors slamming and a loud muffler driving off. I rolled over and pulled my pillow over my head. At 10 PM I was awakened to a loud scream and the building rattling as a flight of jets buzzed the hotel. I got up and noted all the problems I had experienced at the hotel so I could put them in this book. I figured nothing else could go wrong. I was wrong. Starting at midnight and every two hours after that I was treated to trains that had to blow their horns for an extended blast. I was not aware that there was a railroad yard with 12 tracks next to the hotel.

WHY IS IT?

The hotel people always rig my key card so it won't unlock the door to my room and I have to return to the desk to get it re-keyed.

WHY IS IT?

My hotel coffee tastes like it was created last month?

WHY IS IT?

When I travel there is always someone who will speed up, cut in front of you and then travel below the speed limit?

WHY IS IT?

The chairs at the hotels are always too short for the tables?

WHY IS IT?

I always get stuck next to a female who grooms her hair with her fingers, plucking hair follicles out and depositing them next to me?

WHY IS IT?

Some of them crawl off after hitting the floor?

WHY ME?

I was walking down the ramp to the aircraft when I became aware of the woman in front of me. I noticed that she was wearing stretch pants and a light weight jacket. The thing that grabbed my attention was not that she was 400 pounds but instead she had a weggie. (pants wedged in the buttocks) What I observed next could have a place in the book of records. She not only had a wedgie where her stretch pants were a thong but as I watched her rear end reached out and grabbed her jacket. Now the jacket and stretch pants were imbedded in the crevice. As I watched the title of a song came to mind, "You Can't Touch This."

WHY IS IT?

I get stuck on a plane with a sports team who lost a key game and they want to blame me for every miserable second of it?

WHY IS IT?

The toilet paper tears off every two squares?

WHY IS IT?

They place the toilet paper dispenser in such a position that you have to contort to reach it?

WHY IS IT?

When you get water in the tub that is just right, you pull the pin for the shower and the water is too hot or cold?

WHY IS IT?

They place the disabled bar across the wall of the shower in such a way that if your not disabled you will be by the time you are through with your shower?

WHY IS IT?

My room is always cleaned last?

WHY IS IT?

The clean up crew always knocks just after I sit on the throne?

WHY IS IT?

I am always behind a person who wipes his nose the full length of his arm?

WHY IS IT?

Handcuffs can't be brought on a plane but 18 inch knitting needles can?

WHY IS IT?

Large people will eat extremely fattening food and then order a diet drink?

WHY IS IT?

So many people at the airport wear purple socks?

WHY IS IT?

Anyone would paint their toe nails green? Never mind I am at the airport!

WHY IS IT?

I am always next to a guy who reads his news paper in his seat and mine?

WHY IS IT?

My flights always have maintenance holds on them?

WHY IS IT?

After take off the pilot states that they had a major problem with the aircraft but he thinks they got it fixed?

WHY IS IT?

I am always behind some one on the inter-state who drives like their looking for a parking space?

WHY IS IT?

I can leave my location by plane, arrive to my destination before I left and still miss my connecting flight?

WHY IS IT?

Spring break at the airport will destroy any hope you have for the future of the country?

IS THIS FOR REAL?

ROAD SIGNS: "USED COWS FOR SALE"

"TATTOO'S WHILE YOU WAIT"

Can I get a tattoo to go?

WHY ME?

I checked in a nationally known hotel and they seemed to take their old sweet time. I dragged my bags down the long hallway only to find that they had no elevator. Bad knees and all I humped my bags to the top floor room. I slid the computer key in the door and a red light flashed. Again I inserted it and again a red light flashed. I could not leave my bags so I humped them back down and the girl at the desk smiled and asked if there was a problem. I am sweating like a pig and red as a beet but I resisted the urge to drag her across the counter. I explained the problem and she lectured me for five minutes on the proper use of the key card. I told her I did it correctly so she scanned the card and found she had entered the wrong number. She re-keyed the card and called the bell man over. I stated that I could handle it and fought with him to get my card. He pulled away and dashed for the stairs. I humped my bags back up and found the bellman standing there with his hand out stretched. I couldn't believe he wanted a tip when he didn't even help with my bags. I grabbed my key, shook his hand and closed the door behind me. Exhausted, I turned on the air conditioner and went to bed. I began to dream of a gentle stream flowing and the sound was so soothing. I bolted upright when I realized that the stream sound was inside my room. I jumped out of bed and found the floor sloshey with water. The stream of water was running down the wall from the air conditioner. I knew it would be hours before a repair could be made so I put a trash can under the water flow. I picked up the phone to get a 6 am wake up call and found that ants were holding formations on the end table. I returned to bed and all was fine until I became exposed to the Chinese water torturer. I began to hear the drip-drip-drip in the can. I got up and placed a towel in the can and went back to sleep. 42 minutes later the drip-drip-drip was back. By now I was beyond sleep. I began to think that maybe a hot stinging shower would relieve all my stress. I went into the bathroom and prepared for relaxation. I stepped into the shower and adjusted the water temp. to the right setting and then I pulled up on the knob that would re-direct the water over my withering body. To my surprise the knob came off into my hand and the guts fell into the tub. I collapsed into the tub and began mumbling incoherently. I gathered my senses and began to take a shower on my knees.

WHY IS IT?

I go into a major restaurant and the waiter keeps calling me bubba?

WHY IS IT?

When I fly to Florida and the clerk announces "any one who needs extra time to board you can pre-board now" everyone boards leaving me alone in the waiting room?

WHY IS IT?

I get on the elevator that showed the up arrow at the same time as an elderly woman. She hit the down button and I hit the up button. She looked at me indignantly and stated "I Am Going Down." As the elevator went up I looked at her and said "No You Are Going Up." As we reached my floor I hit the down button and turned to her. I then stated "Now You Are Going Down." As the doors closed she screwed up her face and stuck her tongue out.

WHY IS IT?

I am always in the line where someone wants to pay for a hundred dollar item with change?

WHY IS IT?

I am the one the mental picks out to ask for change for a quarter?

WHY IS IT?

It is all sunshine until I arrive at the airport and then it is torrential rain?

WHY IS IT?

They take better care of donor organs being transported by air than passengers?

WHY IS IT?

A passenger moves a briefcase and paper from a chair then when the owner returns she said, "I didn't know anyone was sitting here?"

WHY IS IT?

Indianapolis to Washington/Dulles to Hartford. I load the plane in Indianapolis and they recognize there is going to be a delay because it was raining in Washington. Instead of telling us they pull out to the runway and park. Two hours later they decide to leave. I arrive at Washington/Dulles only to find that they canceled my flight to Hartford. I looked outside and noticed that it was bone dry. I began my odyssey when I was directed to a line at one of the A terminal gates. I stood in line for 20 minutes and watched as the crowd became madder and madder. I finally got my chance to determine how I was going to get to Hartford. They stated they couldn't help me so I needed to go to another A terminal gate. This occurred two more times. Finally the last one told me to go through security and get in line for ticketing. I stood in line for one hour and finally got my chance. I explained that I needed to get to Hartford and they said that the earliest I could get out was on a flight that arrived at 07:50 hours the next day. I explained that I had to be delivering my seminar by 8 am. They just looked at me, tilted their head and looked away. This action reminded me of my miniature Doberman . The woman stated that there was a flight out at 9:50 PM but it was full. She then stated that I could go stand by. I then asked her to put me on stand by and she said that she couldn't because I had to be checked in. I asked her to check me in for the next day flight. She stated she couldn't book me on a next day flight. She told me to go to baggage claim. I stood in line again and the employee stated that I didn't need to get my baggage. He stated he would get it out on the 9:50 PM flight. He then gave me a sheet of paper and stated that it was my ticket for the next morning's flight. I asked are you sure and he stated that I could go to ticketing if I liked. Back to ticketing I went. I stood in line again and got the same women. I showed her the paper from the guy in baggage and she said "What is this?" I told her the story and she said it was not a ticket. I again asked her to book me for the next morning so I could get on stand by. Again she said it couldn't be done. I began to lose it and she found a way to get it done. She printed me off a ticket for the morning flight and I then requested that she put me on stand by for the 9:50 flight. She piddled for a bit then said she couldn't put me on stand by. I then was told to go to gate 11 and they would put me on stand by. Back through security and down into the bowels of hell I went. Again I stood in line and this time I did get on the plane.

After a delay I got into Hartford. When I arrived, guess what, They lost my luggage. My seminar started at 8:30 but I didn't have my clothes or class material until 4:30 PM the next day. I thank god I had a priority rush placed on my bag or I may not have gotten it till I was too old to use it.

WHY IS IT?

Even when they tell us what the snack is, I can't identify it when I eat it?

WHY IS IT?

You ask for a window seat and they say you got it, when you board you find they lied?

WHY IS IT?

They wait till the food cart is next to my seat before they decide to squeeze through?

WHY IS IT?

When I am seated in the exit row and the pilot announces that a famous site is on my side of the aircraft, everyone wants to lean over my seat to look outside?

WHY IS IT?

When you put a rush on a claim to locate your bags, it takes twice as long to find it?

POET'S PLACE

The Perpetual Journey
by Kevin B. Kinnee

Sun pouring down fire
on a parched and desolate land.

No shade or reprieve.

Telltale signs of life
a withered shrub
a shriveled branch
a seared blade of grass.

Nothing living
only past.

Skeletal remains scattered about
by some violent act.

One journey ends
another begins.

A Patriot's Fight
by Kevin B. Kinnee

I'm pleading to our people
to gather around the feet
of the men who founded our country
and the men who made us free.

Let us show our leaders
that this freedom has a price.
It's paid with human suffering
and it's paid with human lives.

Many men have gone before us
and women just the same
to fight to preserve this freedom
and now our dead are shamed.

By allowing these people
who chose not to serve
back into the ranks of our homeland
our freedom we don't deserve.

Freedom is not a given thing
and freedom is not a right
and freedom won't be around us long
if our people are not willing to fight.

These people who left our country
in action stated their views
their not willing to fight for their freedom
and they will never fight for you.

I'll tell you what is going to happen
when a crisis knocks at the door.
These people will leave this country
***AND THE PATRIOTS WILL FIGHT
ONCE MORE!***